Chillin'
trix
for COOL CHIX

Chillin' trix

for COOL CHIX

fab recipes, crafty fun, mystic
magic, and super-cool quizzes

Leanne Warrick

Watson-Guptill Publications/New York

First published in the United States in 2005 by
Watson-Guptill Publications,
a division of VNU Business Media, Inc.
770 Broadway, New York, NY 10003
www.wgpub.com

PRODUCED BY Breslich & Foss Ltd, London
DESIGNED BY Roger Daniels

Special thanks to the cool chix in Watson-Guptill's teen focus group
for their ideas, feedback, and enthusiasm.

Library of Congress Control Number: 2004109746

Printed and bound in China

ISBN 0-8230-4501-3

1 2 3 4 5 6 7 8 / 12 11 10 09 08 07 06 05

Contents

Bust Boredom

Don't you just hate those days when there's *nothing* to do? You're so bored you could cry, and it seems like you're destined to spend the entire day staring out the window or watching TV. Well, look no further—this book is packed with so many cool ideas you won't know what to do first!

Take one of our revealing quizzes to discover the real you, then put on your fortune teller's hat and learn how to predict the future. Is your room is a mess? Can't find anything to wear?

Forever!

We'll show you how to give yourself and your space a whirlwind makeover. Hungry? There are tons of easy, delish recipes to keep your energy up. And if you're itchy for a crafty challenge, there are loads of cute, easy projects you can unleash your creativity on.

Keep this book handy and you'll never again face a day of swatting flies and picking lint off your sweaters. Dive in with your best friends, or get busy on your own for some quality "me" time. Either way, have fun!

Quiz Show

Ever wanted to find out more about yourself, or to work out how well you and your best friend really know each other? How about discovering your perfect perfume, or finding out whether that guy you've been eyeing is eyeing you, too? Now you can get the answers to these and loads more questions thanks to our easy and revealing quizzes. There are a bunch of different types—some to do alone, others with a bud. It's like a complete guide to life! So what are you waiting for? Grab a pencil and get quizzing!

Are You Shy Around Guys?

Do you run away at the mere sight of a boy? Or do you just *love* hanging out with the opposite sex? Check each statement below that describes you, then find the color you checked most. Read the results to find out how confident you really are around guys.

- I often ask boys out.

- If a guy is shy, I might make the first move, but I prefer it if he approaches me first.

- If I feel like talking, I often call a guy friend.

- I will only kiss a boy if he's kissed me first.

- If I like someone, I send out flirty signals to let him know.

- If I get dumped, I know it has something to do with me.

- If I get dumped, it's the guy who has lost out.

- I would NEVER call a guy. I'm way too shy.

- If a boy tells me I look nice, I tell him the same straight back.

- My friends always have to tell me when a guy likes me. I never notice myself!

- If I get dumped, I figure it wasn't meant to be and move on.

- If a guy tells me I look nice, I usually think he's lying.

■ I like dancing with guys, but also with my friends.

■ If I like someone, I'll come right out and tell him!

■ I could never dance with a guy—I'd be too nervous.

■ If a boy tells me I look nice, I say thanks!

■ I *love* dancing with guys.

■ I think about boys some of the time, but I'm not obsessed!

Your score

 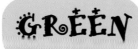 

Wow! You certainly don't need any help when it comes to guys. You have absolutely no problem talking to them, or letting a boy know when you like him. That's great, but some guys might find this a teensy bit scary. Remember that *all* relationships (including friendships) should be equal. Let the guy take the lead sometimes—he'll love you all the more for it!

Hey shy girl! What's holding you back? You are so timid it's almost painful. If you never show guys how amazing you are, how will they ever get to know you? Try opening up and relaxing. Guys are just people like you, after all. The more you do it, the less scary it will seem— before you know it, you'll be as confident as can be!

You have the balance just about perfect! You are comfortable talking to guys and know how to show a boy that you like him—in a subtle way, of course! You've probably got lots of guy friends, and feel comfortable having them around. Take courage though: It sometimes pays to make the first move. Try it and see!

How Well Do You Know Your Best Friend?

Are the two of you best buds, or just casual friends? Answer the questions on the opposite page, then give your friend a pencil and have her fill in the quiz on page 14. Scoring is easy. Just mark the other's form, giving a point for each correct answer. Got your total? Cool. Now read the results and find out how great a friend she really is!

1. If your friend could be any movie star, who would she be?

....

2. What is your bud most afraid of?

....

3. What is her favorite animal?

....

4. What's her favorite candy bar?

....

5. If she was going to treat herself, she'd:
A) Get a new book.
B) Get a double-scoop ice-cream cone.
C) Get a new outfit.

6. Her dream job is:
A) Veterinarian.
B) Actress.
C) Fashion designer.
D) Other:

....

7. If your best friend likes a boy, she:
A) Tells you eventually, but only after you beg her.
B) Tells the entire school—she likes to be open with her feelings.
C) Asks you for advice, then the two of you spend hours planning how to bag that boy!

8. What's the most hilarious thing you've ever done together?

....

9. When she's sad or upset, you know that she:
A) Likes her own space to think things over.
B) Wants you by her side the whole time for support.
C) Wants to be alone for a while, then will come to you when she's good and ready.

10. What's her phone number and e-mail address? Write them here:

....

1. If your friend could be any movie star, who would she be?

....

2. What is your bud most afraid of?

....

3. What is her favorite animal?

....

4. What's her favorite candy bar?

....

5. If she was going to treat herself, she'd:
A) Get a new book.
B) Get a double-scoop ice-cream cone.
C) Get a new outfit.

6. Her dream job is:
A) Veterinarian.
B) Actress.
C) Fashion designer.
D) Other:

....

7. If your best friend likes a boy, she:
A) Tells you eventually, but only after you beg her.
B) Tells the entire school—she likes to be open with her feelings.
C) Asks you for advice, then the two of you spend hours planning how to bag that boy!

8. What's the most hilarious thing you've ever done together?

....

9. When she's sad or upset, you know that she:
A) Likes her own space to think things over.
B) Wants you by her side the whole time for support.
C) Wants to be alone for a while, then will come to you when she's good and ready.

10. What's her phone number and e-mail address? Write them here:

....

Your score

1-3 points

Are you sure you guys know each other? It's great to be independent, but this is ridiculous! Each of you should spend a little more time finding out what makes the other tick, then you'll be far better equipped to support your friend when she needs you.

4-7 points

You guys seem to have the balance just about right. You know each other well enough to be great friends, but realize that she needs her own space once in a while. Make sure you appreciate each other, and you've both got a best friend for life.

8-10 points

Hey, are you sure you are separate people?! It's great to get along, but have you ever thought that you might be a little too close? Make sure you're not closing yourselves off to new friendships. A girl needs all the friends she can get. And that goes for both of you!

Does He Really Like You?

You've been hanging out with this guy for a while now, but how much does he really like you? Guys can be a mystery. Take our test to find out how he truly feels.

1. When you're together and you run into someone he knows, how does he introduce you?
A) "I'd like you to meet my girlfriend."
B) "This is (your name)."
C) He doesn't introduce you.

2. When you go to a party together, how does he act around other girls?
A) He talks to them, but he's never away from your side for long.
B) You barely see him all night. He's too busy flirting with all your friends.
C) He's a really friendly guy, so he spends equal time with you and other people.

3. Your parents invite him over for dinner. How does he act?
A) He says he'll come, but then hardly talks and leaves right after you've finished eating.

B) He seems a little uncomfortable, but then relaxes as the evening goes on.
C) He and your dad get along great. They even make plans to go see a football game together.

4. You have a date and you've spent all afternoon getting ready. What does he say when he sees you?
A) "Wow! You look amazing. I can't believe you made this much effort!"
B) "You look really nice."
C) He doesn't say anything about how you look.

5. It's your birthday, the first one since you've been hanging out. What does he do for you?
A) Nothing. He says he didn't know it was your birthday.
B) He gets you a really cute T-shirt and flowers, and burns a CD of your favorite songs.

C) He buys you a CD you hinted that you'd like.

6. You're sick with flu, and he's dropped by to give you a homework assignment. What does he say when you see him?

A) "Hope you feel better soon. Bye!"
B) "Oh you poor thing! Can I stay and keep you company?"
C) "You look terrible," and then leaves.

Your score

1. A) 3 B) 2 C) 1
2. A) 3 B) 1 C) 2
3. A) 1 B) 2 C) 3

4. A) 3 B) 2 C) 1
5. A) 1 B) 3 C) 2
6. A) 1 B) 3 C) 2

6-9 points
Run away! Fast! Why are you even bothering with this guy? There's only one person he really loves, and that's himself. It would be cool if you were at least having fun together, but it seems he is too selfish to spend time with anyone other than his friends. Cut him loose and fill your life with people who care about you.

10-14 points
You two have a blast together, but as far as romance is concerned, things are just not happening. It's time to take a close look at the relationship. Are you better off as friends? Being just friends means you can still hang out, but you won't be closing yourself off to other cuties. After all, Mr. Right may be just around the corner!

15-18 points
This guy is serious about you! He seems committed to being boyfriend of the year, so make sure you hold on to him! Just one thing: Are you sure you're putting as much into this as he is? If the relationship is one-sided, it's time to start making an effort or move on.

What Does Your Bedroom Say About You?

Are you a control freak or Miss Ultra-Relaxed? Find out here.

START HERE

You spend a lot of time in your bedroom.

TRUE

You often end up spending all of your allowance on stuff for your room.

TRUE

You chose the paint color and the curtains yourself.

TRUE

FALSE

FALSE

Your closet is always a mess and there are clothes and shoes all over your floor.

FALSE

You pick up your room at least once a week.

TRUE

FALSE

FALSE

TRUE

You never look under your bed. You're scared of what you might find!

FALSE

TRUE

When friends come over for the first time, they're impressed by how your room is decorated.

TRUE

FALSE

Perfect Palace
Your friends feel like they're staying at a swanky hotel when they come to your room. In fact they're probably afraid to move in case they knock something over. Your room is your own space, and it's great that you take so much pride in it. Just be careful that you don't become a control freak. It's just a room, after all!

TRUE

You love scented candles and always have one burning when you're there.

FALSE

Cozy Crib
Your room sounds like a fun place to hang out! You like to keep it tidy-ish, but the most important thing is that it feels like you. You have stuff around that some people (like your mom) say looks messy, but to you having these things is a way to personalize your space. Make sure you keep control of the clutter so your room feels calm, not overcrowded.

TRUE

FALSE

You enjoy having friends sleep over in your bedroom.

FALSE

Nightmare Mansion
Eeeek! What happened here? You really do see your room as just a place to crash. You have never bothered to make it a peaceful place, and boy does it show. Harmonizing your room won't take as long as you think, and getting rid of stuff you no longer want or need will make you feel so much better. Get to it!

You can't remember the last time you saw the floor!

TRUE

What's Your Perfect Perfume?

The scent you wear says a lot about you, so it's important to choose one that reflects your personality. Take this simple quiz to find out which "fragrance family" your next perfume should come from, then get shopping!

1. Out of these three, which color do you prefer?
A) Pink. The color of roses and romance.
B) Purple or red. Rich, luxurious colors are best.
C) Yellow. The color of sunshine!

2. What type of weather is your favorite?
A) Rainy and misty. It's so refreshing!
B) Hot, hot, hot! You love the feeling of the sun on your face.
C) Mild and comfortable. Not too hot and not too cold.

3. What's your favorite outfit?
A) Jeans and a cool tee.
B) A black mini and kitten heels.
C) A flowery sundress. The pinker, the better.

4. What would be your dream vacation?
A) A spa trip. Beauty treatments and pampering is your idea of heaven.
B) A week in Paris. All those museums and galleries to enjoy, not to mention the shopping!
C) A beach holiday. Sun, sea, and surf is all you need to feel great!

5. How would your best friend describe you?
A) A sassy go-getter who knows what she wants and isn't afraid to try new things.
B) A funny, easygoing person who loves to have fun, whether on the field or at the mall.
C) A sweet, gentle person who is always there to lend an understanding ear.

6. How do you wear your hair?
A) Loose and flowing. You've had long hair since you were tiny, and it's staying that way!
B) In the latest style. You change your hair almost as often as you change your underwear!
C) Short and fuss-free. You have way better things to do with your time than spend hours in front of the mirror.

7. How is your bedroom decorated?
A) Everything is white and simple. You hate clutter, and besides, the minimal look is what's hot right now.
B) Traditional, with floral print bedding and drapes. Of course, there's the occasional cute boy poster.
C) Very luxurious. Rich colors and fabrics are everywhere, and you have your beloved shoe collection on display.

8. What's your "can't-live-without" beauty product?
A) Glitter lip gloss. It matches your glossy style.
B) Pink blush. You like the fresh, romantic look of rosy cheeks.
C) Lip balm with SPF. You prefer a sporty, healthy look.

Your score

1. A) 4 B) 6 C) 2
2. A) 2 B) 6 C) 4
3. A) 2 B) 6 C) 4
4. A) 2 B) 6 C) 4
5. A) 2 B) 6 C) 4
6. A) 4 B) 6 C) 2
7. A) 2 B) 4 C) 6
8. A) 6 B) 4 C) 2

16–25 points
Sporty scents are perfect for you. Look for any fragrance containing citrus fruits, herbs, green tea, or delicately scented flowers. Crisp, vibrant fragrances match your love of all things outdoorsy and reflect your breezy personality. Cool!

26–35 points
Floral scents suit you best. Pick a perfume containing jasmine, orchid, violet, rose, sandalwood, musk, or vanilla. These gorgeous scents reflect your caring nature and laid-back style. Mmmm!

36–48 points
Sweet and yummy scents made of chocolate, caramel, honey, or vanilla mirror your sassy style. You love all things luxurious, and dressing up for a special occasion is your idea of heaven!

Are You a Drama Queen?

Do you cope with life in a calm and collected way, or does the slightest setback send you screaming about it to everyone you know? Take our test to find out.

1. Your best friend calls at the last minute to cancel plans you've had for weeks so she can go out with a guy. How do you react?
A) Tell her that you're disappointed, but don't guilt trip her too much. After all, she's liked this guy forever.
B) Tell her it's totally fine. You're used to her letting you down.
C) Say "Fine!" and hang up on her. Then give her the cold shoulder until she apologizes.

2. While out shopping, you fall in love with a super-cute top. Annoyingly, the store doesn't have your size. What do you do?
A) Freak out loudly at the sales assistant, telling her that you won't be shopping in that store again. Ever.
B) Ask the sales assistant politely if she would call another store to check if they have your size.
C) Feel disappointed, but decide to keep looking for something else.

3. While rushing to class, you bump right into an extremely cute guy. What is your reaction?
A) Avoid making eye contact and rush off down the hall.
B) Drop your stuff all over the floor, fall over on purpose, and ask him to help you up.
C) Say sorry and flash him your friendliest smile.

4. You get the results back from a test you thought you had aced. They're not good. How do you deal?
A) Throw the test back on the teacher's desk, muttering something about re-grading it as you storm out the door.
B) Barely even flinch. Who cares about the stupid test anyway?

C) Tell your best friend that you're disappointed, but make a mental note to study extra hard next time.

5. You learn that a guy you've liked for a while has just asked another girl out for Saturday night. What's your response?
A) Feel sad, but make plans with your girlfriends on Saturday to take your mind off it.
B) Spend all night on the phone, telling everyone you know how unfair it is, then drag a friend to the same movie so you can spy on them during their date.
C) Don't mention it to anyone and pretend you never liked him to begin with.

6. You overhear a group of girls from your school complaining about a good friend of yours. What do you do?
A) Go straight to your friend and tell her (and everyone else) what they said.
B) Listen, horrified, but decide to keep it to yourself.
C) Give the group your coldest look, then tell your friend that they're not worth her friendship, sparing her the hurtful details.

Your score

1. A) 2 B) 1 C) 3
2. A) 3 B) 2 C) 1
3. A) 1 B) 3 C) 2
4. A) 3 B) 1 C) 2
5. A) 2 B) 3 C) 1
6. A) 3 B) 1 C) 2

6-9 points
You hate any type of conflict, don't you? This is a great way of avoiding hassle, but not a good way to get what you want. Try standing up for yourself a little more and you won't get walked on so much.

10-14 points
You seem to have this pretty much down. If something bad happens, you deal with it and move on, but you also refuse to be a doormat to anyone. This is a great way to be, so keep at it!

15-18 points
Yikes! If you're unhappy about something, the world knows about it! It's great to be so open, but it wouldn't hurt to turn things down a notch. Don't forget that other people have feelings, too!

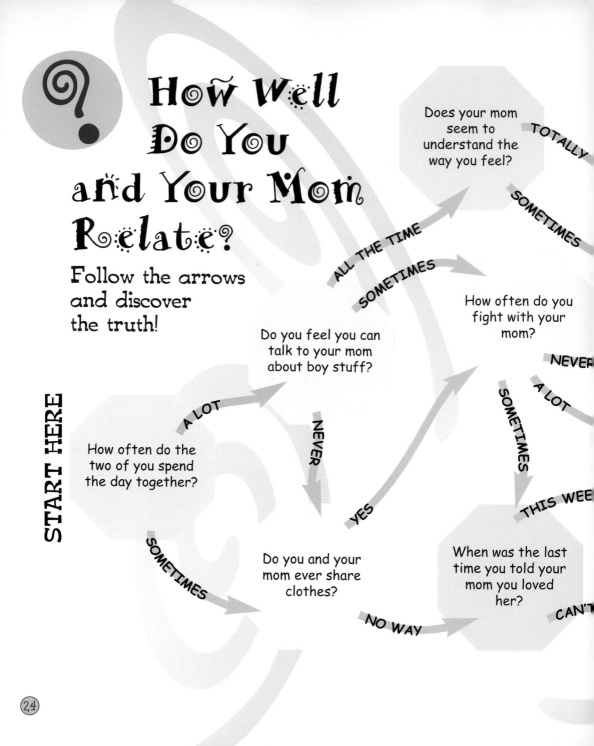

Do you ever help your mom out around the house when she's busy?

ALWAYS

SOMETIMES

NEVER

Aaaaah! You two are more like best buddies than mother and daughter. Your mom gives you advice by the ton, and in return you help her out, too. You know that hanging out with your mom can be fun, and as a result you have a fantastic relationship. Keep up the good work, super-daughter!

Do you think of your mom as a friend?

YES, MY BEST FRIEND

YES

You seem to get on pretty well with your mom, but make sure you let her know how much she means to you. Why not spend a day shopping together, or do a project at home as a team? It will mean she's more likely to understand you when you need her most.

Do you ever surprise your mom with a gift?

SOMETIMES

NO

SOMETIMES

MBER

Does your mom ever ask you for style advice?

It seems you two have a little work to do on your relationship. Sure you love your mom, but it's time to tell her so! Spending time together can be fun, and if it helps you find out more about each other, then even better. Who knows, she could turn out to be the best friend you didn't know you had!

YOU'RE KIDDING!

How Confident Are You?

Self-confidence is super important in every part of life. How much do you think you have, and more importantly, how much do you need? This easy quiz will give you the answer.

1. You run into the guy you've liked for ages at a party, but you also happen to have the world's biggest pimple on your nose. What's your plan?
A) Hang out where the light is most flattering and hope he won't notice the pimple.
B) Leave immediately. He'll never like you if he sees you like this!
C) Go right up and talk to him. Who cares if he's grossed out by a zit? You wouldn't want to be with a superficial guy anyway.

2. Some of your friends are having an argument about something you feel strongly about. You:
A) Say nothing. If you disagree with your friends, they might not want to hang out with you anymore.
B) Express how you feel, but then suggest a change of topic. Nothing is worth ruining friendships over.

C) State your views and refuse to back down, even though the argument is dragging on. You always stand up for what you believe.

3. Your best friend is feeling down and you don't know what the problem is. You feel she might need to talk, but you're not sure. You:
A) Go over to her house—without calling first—to see if she's okay. You figure she needs a good long chat, and you're the gal for the job.
B) Ask her gently if she wants to hang out. If she says no, make her a card to let her know you're there for her, but respect her need for space.
C) Leave her alone. You don't want to bug her or be annoying.

4. When your teacher asks a question in class and looks around for someone to answer, what do you do?

A) If you know the right answer you sometimes speak up—other days you feel a little shy.

B) You never answer! Why would anybody choose to draw attention to themselves?

C) You always speak up. Why not, if you know the answer?

5. You are babysitting for a new family. When they ask for your rate, you:

A) Let them know what you've been paid in the past, then see what they say.

B) Ask for a rate way higher than you've been paid before. After all, if you don't ask, you don't get!

C) Let them set the rate. Even if it's lower than you're used to, it's better than talking about it.

6. You go shopping for something to wear to a party Saturday night. What are you most likely to buy?

A) A new top in a bright color. You love to stand out in a crowd.

B) Another pair of jeans. Who cares if you already have three pairs?

C) A cute skirt from your favorite store. It will go perfectly with a top you already have.

Your score

1. A) 2 B) 1 C) 3
2. A) 1 B) 2 C) 3
3. A) 3 B) 2 C) 1
4. A) 2 B) 1 C) 3
5. A) 2 B) 3 C) 1
6. A) 3 B) 1 C) 2

6–9 points
Why are you so scared of life? It's time to stop caring so much about what other people think and start enjoying yourself! No one wants to look stupid in front of other people, but that's no reason to hold back so much.

10–14 points
You have a pretty cool attitude to life. Sometimes you feel a little quiet, but that's okay. We all have days when we'd rather fade into the background. You are brave enough to speak up for yourself, but not so pushy that quieter people feel intimidated by you.

15–18 points
You are the queen of confidence! Nothing scares you, and you know how to get what you want. This is fine as long as you don't come across as scary, or pushy. Believe it or not, there is such a thing as being too confident!

Style Shake-up

Feel like your sense of style is stuck in a rut? Tired of wearing the same pair of jeans because you can't find anything in the mess that is your closet? Then it's time you had a style shake-up!

Taking a close look at the way you live, and changing things for the better, can make you feel amazing. This section will guide you on a top-to-bottom style makeover. You'll revamp your wardrobe, give your makeup collection a new lease on life, pamper yourself with home-spa treatments, and even turn your bedroom into a stress-free sanctuary. You'll be looking and feeling incredible in no time!

Closet Countdown

How can you put together great outfits if you don't know where half of your favorite stuff is? It's time to reorganize that mess into an easy-to-use boutique of clothes you'll be dying to wear every day. Set aside a day or an afternoon and invite a good friend over to help—someone whose style opinion you *really* trust. When you're done, you can head over to your friend's place and do the same for her!

1. Before you start, get four big boxes or garbage bags and label them "Trash," "Trade," "Keep," and "Customize."

2. Empty all of your clothes and shoes onto the floor in a huge pile. Have your friend make herself comfortable so that she's ready to give you her opinion. Give her a drink or snack and put some music on—it'll help keep your energy up!

3. Try on each item, one at a time. If it doesn't fit you, or you and your friend decide that it doesn't look good, place it in the "Trade" box. If it's stained or ripped beyond repair, put it in the "Trash" box. If an item still fits okay, but you are bored of it, toss it in the "Customize" box. Stuff you still love goes in "Keep."

4. Before doing anything else, get rid of the items in the "Trash" box. Ask a parent or friend if they can use the clothes for cleaning rags or anything else. Otherwise, toss 'em!

GETTING IT TOGETHER

Now it's time to put the stuff from the "Keep" box back into your closet and dresser. Here are some tips to get everything in fashion-friendly order:

♥ Organize clothes into sections, such as pants, cool shirts, sweaters, T-shirts, skirts, exercise clothes, stuff to wear at home, and so on. Invent new categories depending on your lifestyle. Remember, don't put back anything that's not ready to wear right now.

♥ Divide clothes up by color, too. So next time you need a blue T-shirt you can go straight to it, rather than spending 20 minutes getting frustrated looking for it.

♥ Store shoes in their boxes, with a label or picture of what's inside stuck to the outside. This way you can see at a glance where your cute pink sandals or trusty sneakers are hiding.

CLOTHES SWAPPING PARTY

The "Trade" box should be full of clothes you no longer want, but that are still in good shape. Time to organize a party! This is a great way to get rid of things you won't wear anyway, while getting fresh new stuff at the same time. Invite five or more of your best friends over. Tell each one to bring at least five items of clothing that they are bored with.

GET THE PARTY STARTED!

Get the party room ready by setting up chairs or pillows in a circle and a changing area to one side (you can also use a nearby bathroom for changing). When your friends arrive, they should empty their clothes onto the floor. Sort all the stuff into categories, such as casual clothes, dressier clothes, shoes, accessories, and so on.

The hostess of the party (that's you) picks up each item in turn and describes it to the group. For example, you might hold up a skirt and say, "This is a size 5 jean mini from Old Navy." Anyone interested in that item should raise her hand. If more than one person is interested, they all get to try on the item and the others vote on who it suits best.

Remember to be nice—don't shout out things like "Oh, that looks terrible on you!" Make thoughtful comments on how the item fits or whether it looks good on the person.

Have a break halfway through for an energy snack, then finish going through the items.

At the end of the party, you will probably have a pile of clothes and stuff that no one wanted. This should be taken straight to a thrift store so it doesn't end up cluttering your bedroom.

CUSTOMIZING COOL

It's easy to breathe a little life into items you still like, but that seem dated or boring. There are so many ways to unleash your creativity on unwanted items. Go wild! What have you got to lose?

Crafty Cut-offs
Revamp jeans for summer by cutting them off into cute capris. Why not edge the bottoms with pretty ribbon to finish them off? Use fabric glue to fix the ribbon in place.

Tie It Up
Pass a length of ribbon through the arms and neck of a T-shirt to scrunch up the sleeves. Tie the ends in a bow.

Pretty Patches
Patches are simple to sew or glue onto plain tees or pants. Pick some up at the sewing store. Be sure to use fabric glue, which will stay put in the wash.

Button Revamp
Changing the buttons on a coat or jacket can give it a whole new look. Use lots of different colors and styles for a funky feel. Groups of buttons will look cute sewn onto a top, too.

Glitter Girl
Flat-backed rhinestones and gems, fabric glitter spray, and fabric glitter pens are great ways to decorate a plain old T-shirt or pair of jeans. (The instructions on these products will tell you how to wash your glittery clothes.)

Home Spa Day

Who needs to spend money on expensive treatments in swanky spas? You can find everything you need to feel and look fantastic right at home! Just clear your schedule, turn off your cell phone, and prepare to get gorgeous!

Step 1:

SET THE SCENE

Making your bathroom a relaxing place to be is one of the most important parts of preparing your home spa. Clear away clutter and gather everything you need so you won't need to leave the room once you start. Have plenty of clean, fluffy towels and a robe on hand to get the pampered vibe going. Light scented candles and get some of your favorite music to play, too.

Step 2:

BATHING BEAUTY

Your bath should be a treat in itself. Add 2 cups of whole milk to not-too-hot water for a skin softener that will make a real difference. If you have any essential oils in the house, add a few drops to the water to fill the bathroom with a beautiful smell. Lavender or rose would be perfect.

Step 3:

Buffed Bod

Next up, get rid of dead skin cells and give pimples a shock with this smoothing scrub.

1. Mix ½ cup cornmeal and 2 tablespoons fresh or canned pineapple juice in a small bowl.

2. Stand in the tub or shower and massage the scrub onto damp skin using circular motions. Rinse off with warm water and pat yourself with a towel.

Step 4:

Smooth Operator

Smooth olive oil onto your buffed skin while it is still a little damp. This is a great way to seal in moisture all over. Remember to put the towel straight in the laundry basket afterward, as it may be a little oily.

Step 5:

Hair Help

A mashed banana smoothed through your hair will moisturize frazzled locks. Smooth it through washed and towel-dried hair, and leave for ten minutes. This treatment is nourishing for all hair types, but it's especially great if you use a hair dryer and flat irons a lot.

Step 6:

Fruity Face

This fruity mask literally dissolves dead skin cells to leave your face as soft as a peach.

1. Carefully peel ½ of a medium-sized papaya and remove the seeds. With a fork, mash the flesh of the papaya with 1 tablespoon honey in a small bowl.

2. Spread the mixture over your clean face, then lie back and relax for five minutes. This will be plenty of time for the papaya to work.

3. Rinse off with warm water and pat dry. Apply your usual moisturizer.

Step 7:

Cool Eyes

Now that you've washed, buffed, mashed, and moisturized, wrap yourself in a fluffy robe and sit back. It's time to refresh your tired peepers with this soothing eye mask.

1. Slice ¼ of a medium-sized cucumber. Crush the slices with the back of a fork to release the juice.

2. Soak 2 round cotton pads in the cucumber juice. Lay the wet pads over your closed eyelids.

3. Relax for five to ten minutes while the pads cool and brighten your eyes.

Makeup-Bag Makeover

Are you bored with your beauty routine? Have you been using the same products and brushes for months? Sounds like it's time for a makeup bag makeover! Dirty brushes can lead to pimples and other skin problems. It's super important to keep this stuff clean and fresh. After all, it does touch your skin every single day.

1. Start by emptying your makeup bag or drawer and washing it inside and out with warm soapy water. Lay the bag inside out on a towel to dry, or wipe the inside of the drawer. Your brushes should be washed, too. Gently rub the bristles under water to get rid of any old makeup. Squeeze the water out with a towel and leave the brushes out to dry.

2. Dump out all of your makeup onto a table or your bed. Do you actually wear all of it? If you answer no to anything, it's time to trash it.

3. Now look at what's left. How long have you had this stuff? Mascaras should only be used for six months, and NEVER shared with friends as they can cause nasty eye infections. Pencils last longer, as the tips can be sharpened to clean and refresh them. Old lipsticks should be carefully sliced off at the top with a knife. Use clean tissues to wipe off the top layer of powder eye shadows, and give everything a general cleaning by wiping down the packaging.

4. Pay a visit to your nearest department store. This is a great place to try out new colors and get professional advice before you buy. Ask the sales assistants for help.

They are usually happy to give you a mini-makeover, so ask for application tips while they work on you. If you can't afford to buy anything, go straight to your local drugstore, where you can find the colors you liked for a fraction of the cost. Bargain!

5. Promise yourself that you'll do this at least once a season. Keeping your makeup clean and fresh, and your look up-to-date, will help you feel great about yourself every time you use makeup.

Bedroom Bliss

Style isn't only about how you look. It's also about the space you live in. Does your room make you feel good? Or is it a disaster area packed with stuff you never use? Make your room a sanctuary by using some tips from the old Chinese art of *feng shui*. According to feng shui, the way you arrange furniture and other stuff in your room can have an impact on your life. Try these easy tips to maximize your happiness and luck, and add zing to your life!

1. Get rid of clutter. Having loads of stuff lying around can trap negative energy and make you feel down. Clearing out clutter is the single easiest way to get the *chi* (energy) moving in your room and instantly make yourself feel calmer.

2. Think about what pictures and posters you have on your walls. Choose happy images that make you feel good. Photos of fun times and people you love are perfect.

3. Get a crystal. Not only do they look cool, but crystals are great for encouraging the movement of positive chi around your space. Hang one in the window so that it catches the light.

4. Place your desk where you can see out of a window or door for a great studying environment. Your lamp should always be at the south side of your desk.

5. Use color to set the mood of your room. Blue is a calming color, perfect for a bedroom. Red is considered lucky, while green increases vitality. Add color by painting the walls, or by putting a throw or colorful pillows on the bed.

6. Borrow a compass to find out which is the southwest corner of your room. This is your love corner. Never place a wastebasket there! Instead, put a piece of rose quartz

crystal in that spot to energize your love life. In fact, anything pink will encourage love.

7. Open a window. Even in the winter, a ten-minute blast of fresh air in the room will make sure that the chi is kept fresh and full of life.

8. And here's a tip for the bathroom: Always put the toilet seat down! Good energy can escape right down it. No kidding!

Mystic

Ever wanted to try your hand at a little fortune-telling? Do you think of yourself as a mystical, sensitive type? Well, now's your chance to test those supernatural powers!

Fortunes

You'll find plenty of ways in this chapter to sneak a peek into the future and find out more about yourself and your best buds (not to mention your crush). You might get an answer to a question that's been bugging you for ages, or find out something fascinating about your best friend! All of the methods are super simple and a lot of fun to do. One thing's for sure: You'll soon have a line of people desperate to have their fortunes told by you!

It's in the Stars

Your horoscope changes every day, but some stuff about your personality stays the same all year round. Find your star sign, then read on to find out about the real you!

Aquarius
January 21st to
February 19th

Intelligent and always coming up with clever new plans, you are unpredictable and often surprise those around you. Sometimes friends feel like you don't really care about them. Be sure to show them that you do!

Your colors: Silver, aqua, and purple
Your zodiac birthstone: Garnet

Pisces
February 20th to
March 20th

Wow! What a great listener. You are extremely sensitive, so you're the one friends always come to for support. You are very creative, and love to make stuff. You have a tendency to be moody, so keep smiling and you'll be fine!

Your colors: Pale green and purple
Your zodiac birthstone: Amethyst

Aries
March 21st to
April 20th

Confident and fearless, you make a fantastic leader. Just be careful not to overpower less confident people, who might find you a little scary.

Your colors: Red and white
Your zodiac birthstone: Bloodstone

Taurus
April 21st to
May 20th

You are very practical and always know what to do in a crisis. You have a magnetic personality, which means you are always surrounded by friends. You have a tendency to be materialistic, though, so remember—people are more important than things!

Your colors: Brown and turquoise
Your zodiac birthstone: Sapphire

GEMINI
May 21st to June 21st

Quick-witted and ingenious, you always have a plan up your sleeve. You change your mind often, and are easily bored. Beware your gossipy tongue, Gemini, because it could get you in trouble one day!
Your colors: Yellow and light blue
Your zodiac birthstone: Agate

CANCER
June 22nd to July 23rd

A lot of people see you as being tough, as that's how you seem from the outside. But your friends know the real you—underneath that shell, you're really a soft and deep person. You love your home, but you make sure you get out lots, too!
Your colors: White and silver
Your zodiac birthstone: Emerald

LEO
July 24th to August 23rd

Your love of life means you always have lots of friends and are popular. You adore being the center of attention. Be careful not to be overbearing—not everyone is as lively and outgoing as you.
Your colors: Gold and purple
Your zodiac birthstone: Onyx

VIRGO
August 24th to September 23rd

You are a true perfectionist in everything that you do. This is great when it comes to school, but be careful that you're not too critical of your friends. Not everyone is as perfect as you, Virgo!
Your color: Blue
Your zodiac birthstone: Carnelian

LIBRA

September 24th to October 23rd

You love to be admired for your style and taste. Try not to be hurt if someone doesn't notice that you have a new haircut! You are surprisingly determined to get what you want. You go, girl!
Your colors: Ivory and pink
Your zodiac birthstone: Peridot

SCORPIO

October 24th to November 22nd

Sexy and strong, you are fascinated by people and love to find out what makes them tick. Be careful not to let jealousy ruin your friendships, though, as this is a part of your personality. Life is not a competition!
Your colors: Black and red
Your zodiac birthstone: Beryl

SAGITTARIUS
November 23rd to December 22nd

If you want an honest opinion, ask a Sagittarian! You never lie to save anyone's feelings. This is a valuable quality, but beware of hurting the people you love. You love to lead, but don't always give yourself the chance. Push yourself forward the next time an opportunity comes up!
Your colors: Maroon and tan
Your zodiac birthstone: Pink topaz

CAPRICORN

December 23rd to January 20th

You are a loyal friend and will always stick by those you care about. Be careful not to be too possessive over friends, though. That's not the way to keep them. You are very hardworking and will go far in your chosen career.
Your colors: Chocolate brown and navy blue
Your zodiac birthstone: Ruby

Are Your Stars Aligned?

How compatible are you and your crush? Find your star sign on the chart and look down to where his meets yours—that number is your score. Then just read below to see how your match measures up!

Your Love Score

2 Forget it. You guys would have trouble even being in the same room together, let alone dating!

3 No way! You might agree to disagree, but you'll never make it, even as friends. Sorry!

4 You two might get along as friends, but as far as romance goes, it's a no-no.

5 It's not an obvious match, but if you try hard enough, there's a chance it could work.

6 You two will get along great, at least as friends. Whether it ever becomes more than that is another matter.

7 There's definitely hope here! This match has a spark that shows every sign of blossoming into love.

8 Looking good! You guys could definitely have a future together. Good luck!

9 Wow! You two are perfect for each other. Just make sure you're not so loved-up that you forget your friends!

YOUR SIGN

	AQUARIUS	PISCES	ARIES	TAURUS	GEMINI	CANCER	LEO	VIRGO	LIBRA	SCORPIO	SAGITTARIUS	CAPRICORN
AQUARIUS	5	4	8	2	9	3	3	3	9	3	8	3
PISCES	4	5	3	7	4	9	4	5	4	9	4	9
ARIES	8	3	5	5	7	2	8	2	4	4	9	2
TAURUS	2	7	3	3	4	7	4	9	5	4	3	9
GEMINI	9	4	7	4	7	4	8	5	9	3	4	3
CANCER	3	9	2	7	4	5	4	8	4	7	5	5
LEO	3	4	8	3	8	4	4	5	8	3	9	5
VIRGO	3	5	2	9	5	8	5	5	4	8	3	9
LIBRA	9	4	4	5	9	4	8	4	5	4	8	4
SCORPIO	3	9	4	4	3	7	3	8	4	5	3	8
SAGITTARIUS	9	4	9	3	4	5	9	3	8	3	5	5
CAPRICORN	3	9	2	9	3	5	5	9	4	8	5	4

YOUR CRUSH'S SIGN

Which Animal Are You?

Did you know that the year you were born can tell you something about your personality? According to Chinese horoscopes, each year is one of 12 animals. Check the following pages to find the year you were born and which animal you are. And don't stop with yourself. Do the same for friends, family—anyone!!

Rat

Years: 1960, 1972, 1984, 1996
Good points: Active; intelligent; strong-willed; ambitious
Bad points: Stubborn; selfish
Your loves: Having friends over; mysteries; travel
Your hates: Being on your own; alarm clocks; failing
Romance: You need to feel that your boyfriend appreciates you.
Career: You'd make a great storeowner, writer, or musician.

Ox

Years: 1961, 1973, 1985, 1997
Good points: Steady; trustworthy; good planner
Bad points: Set in your ways; hot-headed
Your loves: Saving money; homemade sweets; natural colors
Your hates: Things that are too trendy; bright colors; being taken for granted
Romance: You are easily hurt and cautious in love.
Career: Think about becoming a naturalist, gardener, or chef.

Tiger

Years: 1962, 1974, 1986, 1998
Good points: Enthusiastic; positive; loyal
Bad points: Self-centered; bad-tempered if things go wrong for you
Your loves: Parties; spending money; surprises
Your hates: Being ignored; gossip; feeling trapped
Romance: You love dating . . . but not just one guy!
Career: You would enjoy being a police officer or working in travel—maybe as a pilot or travel agent.

Rabbit

Years: 1963, 1975, 1987, 1999
Good points: Calm; a great host
Bad points: Sometimes too afraid to grab opportunities
Your loves: Romantic movies; long hair; hanging out with friends
Your hates: Arguments; seeing violence; taking risks
Romance: You like spending cozy time with someone special.
Career: Your nature is suited to work as a writer, therapist, or social worker.

DRAGON
Years: 1952, 1964, 1976, 1988
Good points: Giving; charismatic; caring
Bad points: Over-confident; loud; critical
Your loves: Picnics; holidays; fireworks
Your hates: Waiting; dishonesty; being bored
Romance: You attract guys easily but then get bored with them.
Career: Your personality means you'd be a good manager, business owner, or doctor.

SNAKE
Years: 1953, 1965, 1977, 1989
Good points: Great to talk to; confident
Bad points: Bad tempered; often refuses to take advice
Your loves: Dressing up; giving advice; doing good deeds
Your hates: Anything or anyone who's fake; lending money
Romance: You get who you want no matter what it takes!
Career: You would be a good politician or lawyer. Astrology also interests you.

HORSE
Years: 1954, 1966, 1978, 1990
Good points: Independent; interested in others
Bad points: Blab secrets; sometimes too impulsive
Your loves: Dancing; making people laugh; food
Your hates: Silence; being on your own; being told what to do
Romance: You love whirlwind romances.
Career: You would be a good athlete, actress, or architect.

SHEEP
Years: 1955, 1967, 1979, 1991
Good points: Considerate; trustworthy; gentle
Bad points: Over-sensitive; hesitant; nervous
Your loves: Beauty; peace; forgiveness
Your hates: Offending others; being forced to choose
Romance: You are most likely to meet someone special through friends.
Career: You should think about being a designer or working in advertising.

Monkey

Years: 1956, 1968, 1980, 1992
Good points: Good listener; lively; great memory
Bad points: Hold grudges; sometimes vain
Your loves: Practical jokes; helping others; decorating your room
Your hates: Routines; having to rely on others
Romance: Be careful not to be too emotional in love.
Career: The media or public relations would be great areas for you to work in.

Rooster

Years: 1957, 1969, 1981, 1993
Good points: Wise; brave; always put together
Bad points: Critical of other people's appearance; tactless
Your loves: Being tidy; having time alone; dreaming
Your hates: Losing your cool
Romance: Once you've found Mr. Right, you will be 100% committed.
Career: You would make a good author, entertainer, or stylist.

Dog

Years: 1958, 1970, 1982, 1994
Good points: Sensitive; loyal; reliable
Bad points: Pessimist; worrier
Your loves: Mystical stuff; writing letters; silver jewelry
Your hates: Dishonesty; selfishness
Romance: It takes a while for you to trust someone.
Career: You would be an amazing teacher or doctor.

Pig

Years: 1959, 1971, 1983, 1995
Good points: Honest; affectionate; peaceful
Bad points: Hard to get to know
Your loves: Celebrities; reading; working as a team
Your hates: Arguing; feeling confused
Romance: You need to be sure you have found the right person.
Career: Your creative nature would make you a good gardener or musician.

Your Life in Your Hands

Did you know that you can tell a lot about a person just by studying the palm of their right hand? This practice is known as palmistry, and people have been doing it for hundreds of years. It's simple and fun, so give it a go! Read your own hand first, so you know what the lines mean.

Life Line

Study the shape and curve of the Life Line, then compare it to the diagram to see which color it most resembles. This will tell you what type of life the person whose hand you are reading will have.

Red You are an adventurer and will travel a lot in your life. Once you have left home, you won't go back and live there again.

Purple You adore being outside and enjoying wide-open spaces, but your home is also very important to you.

Blue You are creative and romantic. Your imagination will take you far.

Green You are a delicate sort of person. You love your home and prefer to stay close rather than travel far away.

Heart

Head

LIFE

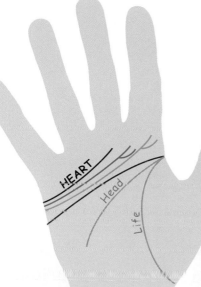

Heart Line

The Heart Line can reveal a lot about who you are when it comes to love.

Red You are a passionate person. Be careful not to put your needs before those of others.
Blue You are warm and generous when it comes to love. You have the balance just right.
Green Be careful not to be superficial in love. You have a tendency to choose a partner by how cool/cute/rich he is!
Purple You love romance, but beware of jealousy in your relationships. It will cause nothing but trouble.

Head Line

Compare the Head Line to the diagram and see what type of person you really are.

Purple Very intelligent, you worry about the world and want to make it a better place.
Red You are incredibly confident. This is a great attribute, but be careful not to rush decisions.
Blue Independence is your best quality. What's more, you are always looking on the bright side of life and don't need anyone to guide you.

Decode Your Dreams

Do you ever wake up wondering what on earth your dream was all about? To understand dreams properly, keep a notebook and a pencil by your bed and write down your dreams as soon as you wake up. If you don't, it's surprising how quickly you'll forget them. Later on, check the list below and on pages 58–59 for things that were in your dream. Good luck!

Airplane If you're scared of flying, an airplane could mean you're trying to figure something out. If you love to fly, this dream means adventure.

Alarm clock You feel that time is running out in one area of your life.

Balding If you lose your hair in your dream, you are worried about illness.

Bear Someone in your life has a bad temper!

Camping It's time to get back in touch with nature.

Cars You feel that whoever was driving the car in your dream has control of your life.

Dancing You are looking for love.

Death This means a new beginning in your waking life.

Eating If you dream about eating, you should try to relax about something you have been very worried about.

Elephant Something important in your life has been forgotten.

Fences You feel separated from someone or something.

Fire Dreaming of fire means that you are struggling to be in control of something. Try to think what that might be.

Garden If it's an overrun, messy garden, you have a low image of yourself. If the garden is well kept, you think highly of yourself.

Ghost This represents something or someone that is gone but not forgotten. They (or it) are still on your mind.

Hat Wearing a hat in your dream means that you feel powerful.

Helicopter You want to be whisked away!

Laughing To laugh in a dream means that you're letting out deep emotions.

Lying You feel ashamed of something in your waking life.

Mirror This is a gateway to a mystical world. Your imagination is running wild!

Money This represents the giving and receiving of power. What is happening to the money in your dream? This will give you a clue as to its meaning.

Nagging If someone in your dream is nagging you, it means you are in denial about something.

Nudity Dreaming that you are naked shows that even confident people—like you—can be shy.

Ocean You are feeling very creative.

Owl This means knowledge. Listen to what the owl says!

Public speaking You feel people are snooping into your daily life to find out something you want to hide.

Quitting To quit at something in your dream means that you're not happy with the way things are going.

Royalty If you dream of royalty, you are hoping for more power in your life.

Running This is a symbol for health and vitality. To dream of running means you're in good shape!

Separation The way you react in your dream to being separated from someone shows your true feelings about that person. Were you upset about being separated, or did it not bother you?

Team sports You long to be a sports legend in real life!

Teeth To lose your teeth in a dream means that you are afraid of embarrassment.

Ugliness If you dream that you are ugly, it's time to boost your self-esteem!

Underwater You long to escape the real world!

Violence If you are aggressive in a dream, it means that you feel frustrated in real life.

Vulture If you see a vulture in your dream, it can mean that you sometimes feel lonely.

Walking If you dream of walking, it means that you should take more notice of how you *get* to places in real life, not just the destination! It could be that you are making life more complicated than it needs to be.

Wedding You are entering into some kind of commitment in your life. The way the wedding happens in your dream might tell you how the commitment in your waking life will go.

X-Rays You long to know someone's innermost thoughts!

Zebra You feel like you have two different personalities in your waking life.

What's in a Name?

According to the science of numerology, the numbers in your life can tell you a lot about who you are. The simplest numerology test is to turn your name into a number, which you can then use to figure out your personality. Try it on your own name, then try the names of your family and friends, and even your crush. Math has never been so much fun!

1. Write down your first and last names. For each letter, look at the table below to find the number above it. Write the numbers down. For example, someone named Ann Smith would be:

Ann: **1, 5, 5**
Smith: **1, 4, 9, 2, 8**

1	2	3	4	5	6	7	8	9
A	B	C	D	E	F	G	H	I
J	K	L	M	N	O	P	Q	R
S	T	U	V	W	X	Y	Z	

2. Now add the numbers for each name together:
  Ann: $1 + 5 + 5 = 11$
  Smith: $1 + 4 + 9 + 2 + 8 = 24$

3. Next, break each answer into individual digits. Add those together:
  Ann: $11 = 1 + 1 = 2$
  Smith: $24 = 2 + 4 = 6$

4. Add the two numbers you ended up with together, giving you one number for your whole name.
  Ann Smith: $2 + 6 = 8$

5. If you wind up with a double digit, like 24, break it apart and add each digit together until you have a single number (so if it was 24, you'd add $2 + 4 = 6$). Now see what it all means!

If your number is:

1 You are ambitious and don't like anyone telling you what to do. You will go far in your chosen career.

2 You are supportive and always know what to say at exactly the right time. You love to analyze people and situations, and you are a great friend.

3 You are always smiling and love to look on the bright side of life.

4 You are practical and can always think of a solution to even the worst situation.

5 You are fascinated by the mystical world and love to explore. You will travel a lot during your life.

6 You are caring and are always looking out for your buds. People are naturally drawn to you for support.

7 You are a very calm and spiritual person. You like to spend time on your own—some people think you're a bit eccentric!

8 You know what you want and are great at making decisions. Be careful not to come across as pushy.

9 Some people are jealous of you because you seem so good at everything! But don't worry, when they get to know you they'll realize that you are a very caring person.

Your Future in a Cup of Tea

The next time you enjoy a hot drink with a friend, make it a cup of tea. You'll get more than just a refreshing treat—you'll get a peek into the future, too! Tea-leaf reading is a way of telling fortunes by seeing shapes in the leaves and "reading" their meanings. The art of tea-leaf reading has been practiced around the world for more than a thousand years. It is thought to have originated in China, where tea was first cultivated. Give it a try!

To read tea leaves you'll need to use loose-leaf tea; put it into a mug and then pour in hot water. If you don't have loose-leaf tea, split open a teabag to let the leaves out and use that. To read someone's future, wait until they have finished their drink. Ask them to leave a tiny bit of tea in the bottom of the cup. Then follow these easy instructions.

1. Hold the cup in your hand and swirl the liquid around the base of the cup three times.

2. Turn the cup upside down onto a saucer. Leave it like this for one minute to let the liquid drain away.

3. Turn the cup right side up, with the handle pointing toward you.

4. You're ready to start reading! Work clockwise around the cup, starting at the handle. Any symbols you see on the left side tell about the past. Those found on the right side will happen in the future.

5. Decode what you see with the easy guide to symbols on pages 64–65.

Anchor You'll soon find an answer to a problem.

Arrow If it's pointing up, it means good luck. If it's pointing down, it means a plan may go wrong.

Bee Beware of gossip.

Bird Good news is coming.

Cat There will be good fortune at home.

Cherry This is the symbol for love, either in your future or your past.

Door You will miss an opportunity.

Dragonfly New clothes are on the way!

Egg More money will soon be yours.

Eye Something needs closer investigation.

Face Change is coming in your life.

Flower Great joy will come soon.

Genie A wish could come true. Be careful what you wish for!

Guitar Music could lead to love!

Hand A new friend will help you.

Hat A visitor may arrive with a gift.

Heart Love is coming!

Insect You will be worried about something.

Ivy Friends will be honest with you.

Jellyfish Beware of a fake person in your life.

Key You will soon have a new passion in your life.

Kite Take a chance!

Lamb You are a shy person.

Leaf Good health and great fortune are on the way.

Man You will have a male visitor.

Moon A love affair will either begin or end.

Nail Someone has been unfair to you.

Necklace Someone in your family will change your future.

Onion A secret is about to be revealed.

Owl There will be sad news that makes you wiser.

Palm tree You will be very creative soon.

Pear All of your hard work will pay off.

Queen You'll meet a special woman.

Question mark Act with care.

Rainbow Everything will get better.

Ring Long-lasting friendship or love is on the way!

Scissors Get rid of the old to make way for the new.

Shoe Someone will show his or her true colors.

Telephone You'll receive an important phone call.

Tree You will reach a goal.

Umbrella You'll receive a generous gift.

Unicorn You may have psychic powers!

Vase A friend will ask for advice.

Violin Someone you know is always complaining.

Wasp You may have difficulties with friends.

Wheel Travel is on the horizon.

Yacht Your money worries are over.

Zipper Be fair in love.

Snack

If you've worked up an appetite, you've come to the right place. This section is full of delish snacks and drinks to mix up and munch with friends. They're all easy to make—some need just a few minutes in the microwave, others don't need any cooking at all.

Before you get cookin', check out these important safety tips:
- Always get permission from an adult before using the kitchen.
- Use pot holders or oven mitts when removing anything from the microwave.
- Ask for help when chopping fruit or vegetables.
- Protect your clothes with an apron.
- Wash your hands before touching any food.
- Clean and put everything away when you're finished.

Chocolate Dippers

Fruit dipped in chocolate is easy to make, looks impressive, and is totally yummy. And since fruit is involved, it *must* be good for you, right? It's best to use fruit that is easy to hold, like grapes, strawberries, or cherries. If you're using larger fruit, like a banana or apple, cut it into bite-sized pieces first. And don't stop with fruit! You can also dip pretzels, potato chips, cookies, dried fruit—basically anything that will hold its shape and taste good covered in chocolate.

You will need:

- strawberries, cherries, bananas, or any other fruit, plus pretzels, cookies, marshmallows, and/or dried fruit such as apricots
- 1 cup semi-sweet chocolate chips
- microwave-safe bowl
- wooden spoon
- cookie sheet
- wax paper
- for decoration: sprinkles, white or dark chocolate flakes, shredded coconut, tiny chocolate chips, or anything else you can sprinkle on top

1. Rinse the fruit in water, then pat dry with paper towels. The fruit must be completely dry or the melted chocolate won't stick to it. Cut larger fruit into pieces.

2. Cover the cookie sheet with wax paper.

3. Place the chocolate chips in the bowl and microwave on high for 1 ½ minutes . Carefully take out the bowl and stir. If the chocolate isn't completely melted, microwave on high for 30 more seconds. Take it out, stir, and if it's still not melted, microwave on high for an additional 20 seconds. Be careful not to overcook or you may burn the chocolate.

4. Dip your pieces into the chocolate, one at a time. After dipping, hold each piece over the bowl until any extra chocolate has dripped off, then place it onto the wax paper.

5. Sprinkle the chocolate-covered piece with your favorite decoration before the chocolate sets.

6. Keep going with your other pieces. When you're done, place them in the fridge for ten minutes or so until the chocolate hardens.

Flower Ice Bowl and Cubes

This flower ice bowl is perfect for a party, whether for two or twenty. And the best part is that you don't need to clean it—you just let it melt! The ice cubes are great for cold drinks on a hot summer day. As they melt, they drop their little petals and herbs into your drink for added flavor. If you're making the ice bowl for a party, start it five or six hours before your guests arrive.

For the flower bowl you will need:

- 1 small handful fresh rose petals
- 1 small handful fresh mint leaves
- 2 bowls, one a little smaller than the other so that it fits inside. (The smaller bowl should allow about an inch of space between it and the larger bowl.)
- vegetable oil or nonstick cooking spray
- cold water
- fresh fruit for eating

1. Rinse the rose petals and mint in water to clean.

2. Pour a little oil onto a paper towel and rub it all over the *inside* of the large bowl and the *outside* of the small bowl. Or spray both surfaces with nonstick cooking spray.

3. Drop the rose petals and mint leaves into the larger bowl. Pour cold water into the bowl until it reaches a third of the way up.

4. Place the smaller bowl inside the larger one so that the water and mint/rose petals are sandwiched between them. (If you're using plastic bowls, put something heavy in the smaller bowl to hold it down.)

5. Put the bowls in the freezer. Leave for about five hours or until the water is frozen.

6. Wait until just before your guests arrive. Then take the bowls out of the freezer. Leave at room temperature for a few minutes, until the ice just begins to thaw. Very gently pull the bowls apart to reveal your ice bowl.

7. Wipe off the oil and put the ice bowl on a plate. Fill with fresh fruit and bring out immediately. The ice bowl will melt eventually, but it will certainly see you through dessert!

For the ice cubes you will need:

- 1 small handful edible flower petals (rose, pansy, marigold, and nasturtium are some examples) or herbs (mint is especially nice)
- ice cube tray
- cold water

1. Rinse the petals or herbs in water to clean.

2. Make sure the ice cube tray is clean and empty. Place one or two petals or leaves into each ice cube compartment.

3. Carefully fill the ice cube tray with water.

4. Place the tray in the freezer for two to three hours or until frozen.

5. Put a cube or two into each glass. Fill with your favorite drink, and serve!

Super Smoothies

Mix up some delicious, nutritious smoothies using one of the recipes below. Just put all ingredients into a blender or food processor and blend until smooth. Pour into a chilled glass and drink!

Orange Smoothie
1 cup milk
1 cup orange juice
2 tablespoons sugar
2 scoops vanilla ice cream

Orange and Banana Smoothie
2 cups orange juice
1 banana, sliced

Strawberry Smoothie
10 oz. strawberries, either fresh or frozen and thawed
4 cups milk
2 cups strawberry ice cream

Fruit Cocktail Smoothie
1 can fruit cocktail, strained
1 cup orange juice
1 cup cranberry juice

Raspberry Peach Smoothie
1 cup peeled and sliced peaches, either canned or fresh
2 cups milk
1 cup frozen raspberries, thawed
1 teaspoon almond flavoring

EACH RECIPE MAKES 3 SMOOTHIES

Popcorn Heaven

These popcorn recipes are super easy to make and perfect for munching. You're guaranteed to get sticky making them, though, so protect your clothes with an apron before you start mixing.

NUTTY POPCORN BARS

You will need:

- vegetable oil or nonstick cooking spray
- 13- x 9-inch baking pan
- knife
- ½ cup dried fruit (such as cherries, apricots, or raisins)
- 6 cups mini marshmallows
- 1 cup semi-sweet chocolate chips
- 6 tablespoons butter or margarine
- large microwave-safe bowl
- wooden spoon
- 10 cups popped popcorn (or 1 bag of popped microwave popcorn)
- 1 cup salted peanuts
- 1 teaspoon vanilla extract

1. Pour a little oil onto a paper towel and rub lightly over the baking pan to grease it. Or spray the pan with nonstick cooking spray.

2. Cut the dried fruit into small pieces.

3. Place the marshmallows, chocolate chips, and butter or margarine in the bowl. Microwave on high for 1 ½ minutes. Remove the bowl and stir. Return to microwave and cook on high for another 30 seconds. Take out and stir. Keep cooking for 30-second intervals and stirring until the mixture is melted and smooth.

4. Stir in the popcorn, peanuts, and vanilla extract. Leave to cool for one minute. Scrape the mixture into the greased pan, using your hands to press the mixture down. (To keep the mixture from sticking to your hands, first wet them with clean, cold water.)

5. Gently press the chopped dried fruit onto the surface of the mixture.

6. Leave to cool at room temperature for about an hour. Cut into 12 to 15 bars and arrange on a plate.

CINNAMON POPCORN BARS

You will need:

- vegetable oil or nonstick cooking spray
- 13- x 9-inch baking pan
- 6 tablespoons butter or margarine
- 6 cups mini marshmallows
- wooden spoon

- large microwave-safe bowl
- 10 cups popped popcorn (or 1 bag of popped microwave popcorn)
- 1 teaspoon cinnamon

MAKES
12-15
BARS

1. Pour a little oil onto a paper towel and rub lightly over the baking pan to grease it. Or spray the pan with nonstick cooking spray.

2. Combine the butter or margarine with the marshmallows in the bowl. Microwave on high for 1 ½ minutes, then stir. If the mixture needs further melting, microwave on high for 30 seconds at a time, then stir, until the mixture is smooth.

3. Add the popcorn and cinnamon to the marshmallow mixture and stir until the popcorn is coated. Scrape into the greased pan, using your hands to press the mixture down. (To keep the mixture from sticking to your hands, first wet them with clean, cold water.)

4. Leave to cool at room temperature for about an hour. Then cut into 12 to 15 bars and arrange on a plate.

CARAMEL POPCORN

You will need:

- vegetable oil or nonstick cooking spray
- 13- x 9-inch baking pan
- ⅓ cup butter or margarine
- ⅓ cup corn syrup
- ⅔ cup brown sugar
- large microwave-safe bowl
- wooden spoon
- ¼ teaspoon baking soda
- ½ teaspoon cinnamon
- 10 cups popped popcorn (or 1 bag of popped microwave popcorn)

1. Pour a little oil onto a paper towel and rub lightly over the baking pan to grease it. Or spray the pan with nonstick cooking spray.

2. Put the margarine or butter in the bowl and microwave on high for 45 seconds. If it's not melted, microwave on high for ten seconds at a time until melted.

3. Remove the bowl from the microwave. Stir in the corn syrup and sugar and mix well. Microwave the whole mixture on high until the mixture begins to bubble (about 1 ½ minutes).

4. Carefully remove the bowl and stir. Microwave on high for another three minutes, then stir in baking soda and cinnamon.

5. Add the popcorn and stir. Then microwave on 70 percent power for one more minute.

6. Stir once more to completely coat the popcorn, then pour the mixture into the greased baking pan and let cool at room temperature for about an hour. Break into bize-size pieces and serve.

Energy Balls

Try these chewy balls for a quick pick-me-up. They're full of delicious, healthy things like dried apricots and honey. Yum!

You will need:

- kitchen scissors
- 12 to 15 dried apricots
- ¼ cup honey
- ⅛ cup vegetable oil
- microwave-safe bowl
- microwave-safe plate or tray
- wooden spoon
- ½ cup rolled oats
- ¼ cup peanuts (optional)
- tablespoon

MAKES ABOUT **15** BALLS

1. Using kitchen scissors, cut the apricots into tiny pieces.

2. Combine the honey and vegetable oil in the bowl. Microwave on high for 30 seconds. Stir well.

3. Add the apricots, oats, and peanuts (if using) to the mixture. Stir again.

4. Drop tablespoonfuls of the mixture a couple of inches apart on the plate or tray. Microwave on high for 30 seconds to "cook."

5. Leave the balls at room temperature to cool and solidify before serving.

Rocky Road Pie

It's hard not to eat this fabulous, frothy, gooey mixture before you freeze it. But be patient—it's even better fresh out of the freezer and slightly melted at room temperature.

For the piecrust you will need:

- 20 graham cracker squares
- large plastic baggie
- rolling pin
- dish towel
- 6 tablespoons butter
- 3 tablespoons sugar
- microwave-safe bowl
- wooden spoon
- 9-inch round pie tin or plate

1. Place the graham crackers in the baggie. Hold the top of the baggie closed with one hand and use the other hand to crush the crackers by smacking them with the rolling pin. (Protect your kitchen counter with a clean dish towel before you do this.) You are done when all you have in the baggie are crumbs.

2. Place the butter in the bowl and microwave on high for 1 ½ minutes until melted. If the butter isn't all melted, microwave on high for 15 seconds at a time until it is.

3. Add the graham cracker crumbs and sugar to the butter. Mix well.

4. Press the mixture into the pie tin, completely covering the bottom and sides. Leave it in the fridge while you make the filling.

For the filling you will need:

- 1 ½ cups half and half nondairy creamer
- large bowl
- 1 package chocolate pudding mix
- whisk
- spatula
- 3 ¼ cups whipped cream topping
- ⅓ cup semi-sweet chocolate chips
- ⅓ cup mini marshmallows
- ⅓ cup cashew nuts

1. Pour the half and half into the bowl. Add the chocolate pudding mix and beat with whisk until blended.

2. Using the spatula, fold in the whipped topping, chocolate chips, marshmallows, and cashews. Blend together with the spatula.

3. Pour the filling into the prepared piecrust. Place in the freezer for at least two hours before serving.

Easy Baked Potatoes

Potatoes are the perfect meal—they're full of vitamin C and are good sources of fiber. They are also a great base for whatever you most like to eat in the world! Follow the directions below for making microwaved baked potatoes, then choose a topping from page 83. Or set up a "toppings bar" and let each person choose for him- or herself!

You will need:

- 1 large potato per person (you can cook 3 to 4 at once)
- fork
- knife
- pot holder or oven mitts

1. Scrub the potatoes clean and carefully prick them all over with a fork.

2. Place them directly onto the microwave shelf or plate.

3. Microwave on high for four minutes. Using oven mitts, turn the potatoes over. Microwave on high for three more minutes.

4. To check whether or not a potato is ready, stick a fork into it. If the fork goes in easily, the potato is cooked. If it isn't quite done, microwave on high for 30 seconds at a time until it's soft.

5. Using oven mitts, remove the potatoes. Cut them in half and add your topping.

Pretend It's Pizza
Cover the potato with your favorite spaghetti sauce and cheese. Microwave on high for 60 seconds to heat.

Mexicana Mama
Pour black beans and grated cheese over the potato, then top with a spoonful of salsa. Microwave on high for 60 seconds to heat.

Just Say Cheese
Sprinkle the potato with one or more kinds of grated cheese. Microwave on high for 30 seconds or until the cheese is melted.

Simply Stuffed
Scoop the flesh of the potato out of the skin and put it into a bowl. Put a tablespoon of margarine or butter, a splash of milk or cream, and salt and pepper into the bowl to taste. Mix it all together, then refill the potato skin.

Light and Healthy
Smother your potato in salsa—the hotter the better!

Almost Salad
Top the potato with grated carrots, sliced tomatoes, garlic salt, and plain yogurt.

Crafty Creations

Got a little time on your hands? Fingers itching to do something besides instant messaging your friends? These cool, easy projects are a snap to make and use supplies you probably have lying around the house. Invite a friend over, whip up some snacks (see pages 66-83), and get busy! Or, if peace and quiet is what you're after, put on your favorite tunes and enjoy some crafty solo time.

Friendship Collage

Here's an arty way to keep memories alive and kickin' on your bedroom wall. If you have a digital camera and a printer, take pictures of you and your friends hanging out, or at an event like this thirteenth birthday party. Or just gather together photos and mementos you already have.

TIME IT TAKES:
About an hour

You will need:

- photos and mementos
- colored poster board
- construction paper
- scissors
- glue stick
- craft glue
- colored paint pens or markers
- extra items for decoration, such as glitter, rhinestones, ribbons, fabric, feathers, magazine cut-outs, fortune cookie messages, fake flowers, buttons—anything that reminds you of the friends or good times in the photos
- paper towels

1. Gather together the photos and mementos. If you don't want to cut the photos, take them to your local copy shop and make color photocopies.

2. Lay the poster board flat. Cut out shapes from the construction

paper to make
an interesting background.

3. Arrange the photos and
mementos on the background. Move
them around until you like the way
they look.

4. Without disturbing your design,
pick up each photo, one at a time,
and use the glue stick to glue it
down. Use craft glue for the bigger
3-D objects. Try leaving some pieces
(like the fortune cookie messages
used here) loose at the ends so the
collage has some texture. Use paper

towels to wipe
off any extra glue. Let dry.

5. Now go crazy! Glue on
rhinestones, flat-backed gems,
flowers, feathers—anything that
reminds you of the friends or events
in your photos. Add doodles with
glitter and metallic paint pens. Draw
dialogue bubbles or buy the ones
used for photo albums to add funny
words and sayings. Use your
imagination—the sky's the limit!
When you're done, let dry overnight.

Best-Friend Bracelets

Make a bunch of these for your best buds in their favorite colors. They can be worn as bracelets, or made slightly longer for anklets.

BRAIDED BEAUTY

You will need:

- 3 strands of thin satin ribbon in different colors, each 15 in. (40cm) long
- safety pin

1. Tie the three strands of ribbon together in a knot about 3 in. (8cm) from one end.

2. Push a safety pin through the knot, and pin it to an old pillow or the knee of your jeans so you can keep the ribbons taut.

3. Here's how to braid: Pass the left-hand ribbon (pink) over the middle ribbon (red) and under the right-hand ribbon (turquoise).

4. Now repeat step 3, starting with the new left-hand ribbon.

5. Continue braiding until the bracelet is long enough to tie around your friend's wrist. Secure with a knot and trim the ends.

Beaded Bling-Bling

You will need:

- 1 strand of embroidery thread for knotting, 60 in. (150cm) long
- 2 strands of embroidery thread for the core, each 20 in. (50cm) long
- safety pin
- beads

1. Tie all three strands in a knot at one end.

2. Push a safety pin through the knot, and pin it to an old pillow or the knee of your jeans so you can keep the threads taut.

3. Hold the core threads in your right hand and the knotting thread in your left. Bring the knotting thread under the core threads, around to the top, and back through the loop you have made. Pull this loop tight to the top of the threads.

4. Repeat step 3. Keep going until your bracelet is long enough. The knots will start to twist as you work.

5. Every so often, slide a bead onto the core threads and continue knotting in the usual way. The bead will become knotted into the bracelet.

6. Finish by tying a knot at the end of the bracelet. Tie the bracelet around your wrist or ankle and trim off the ends.

Chunky Jewelry

Do you or your **Mom** have a drawer full of jewelry that you no longer wear? Rather than letting your treasures collect dust, use them to create gorgeous new pieces. Here are two ideas for putting colorful old beads to good use—a long beaded necklace and a funky, colorful pendant.

TIME THEY TAKE:
About ten
minutes

For each design you will need:

- piece of leather twine, ribbon, or thick thread, 40 in. (1 meter) long
- assorted beads

To make a long beaded necklace:

1. Arrange the beads on a table. Move them around until you find a pattern you like.

2. Decide where you want the first bead. Make a knot in that place on the twine. Slide the bead onto the twine, stopping at the knot. Make a second knot on the other side of the bead to keep it in place.

3. Move down the twine and do the same thing for another bead. Keep going until you've added all of the beads.

4. Knot the ends of the twine together and slide over your head to wear.

To make a beaded pendant:

1. Arrange the beads you want to use on a table. Move them around until you find a pattern you like.

2. Thread the first bead onto the twine. Hold the two ends of the twine and let the bead fall to the center. Tie a knot over the bead to fix it in place.

3. Pass *both* ends of the twine through the rest of the beads, one at a time. Pull them down to rest on top of the first bead. Tie a knot to keep them in place.

4. Make sure that you leave at least 13 in. (33cm) of twine so that you can slip the pendant over your head. Tie a knot in the free end of the twine, and the pendant is ready to wear.

Funky Frame

This is a quick and easy way to turn a plain picture frame into something special. Make sure that you make the cardboard frame bigger than the original one to cover it completely.

TIME IT TAKES:
About half an hour

You will need:

- plain picture frame
- piece of cardboard larger than the frame
- pencil
- ruler
- scissors
- paint
- paintbrush
- strong glue (to attach the cardboard to the frame)
- craft glue
- glitter
- things to decorate your frame, such as glitter glue, gems, rhinestones, stickers, magazine cut-outs, etc.

1. Lay the picture frame in the center of the piece of cardboard and trace around it. Then, measure the width of the frame edge and mark that on the cardboard, too.

2. Now draw a new frame, using the traced frame as a guide. You can make the edges curved, squiggly, zig-zag—however you want. If the frame will sit on a table, make the bottom even so it won't fall over.

3. Cut out the new frame, including the center (where the picture will go). Paint it, then leave to dry.

4. Glue the cardboard frame to the original picture frame.

5. Decorate your frame by gluing on glitter and other decorations. You can also use paint pens to add doodles or sayings. It can be as elegant or as crazy as you want! Let dry overnight, then insert your favorite picture.

Memory Journal

Transform a plain notebook into this romantic journal for your secret thoughts and memories. Use any image of your favorite celeb and surround it with flowers and "diamonds."

You will need:

- pink notebook
- silver stick-on sequins or glitter glue
- scissors
- pictures of your favorite celeb and flowers
- glue stick

TIME IT TAKES:
About half an hour

1. Line three edges of the notebook cover with stick-on sequins or glitter glue.

2. Arrange the pictures on the notebook.

3. When you are happy with the design, pick up each image, one at a time, and glue it onto the notebook. Let dry.

4. Fill your new journal with notes, thoughts, and dreams!

index